THE GOSPEL

MUSIC FROM THE MOTION PICTURE SOUNDTRACK

ISBN 1-4234-1206-0

HAL•LEONARD®
CORPORATION

7777 W. BLUEMOUND RD. P.O. BOX 13819 MILWAUKEE, WI 53213

Visit Hal Leonard Online at
www.halleonard.com

HE REIGNS

Words and Music by
KIRK FRANKLIN

God is an awe-some God. He reigns from Heav-en a-bove with_ wis - dom pow'r and love. Our

God is an awe-some God. Our God is an awe-some God. He _ reigns from Heav-en a-bove with

wis - dom pow'r and love. Our God is an awe - some God.

VICTORY

Words and Music by
GREGORY CURTIS

I got, got the vic-to-ry. I got the sweet, sweet vic-t'ry in Je - sus. Yes, I do.

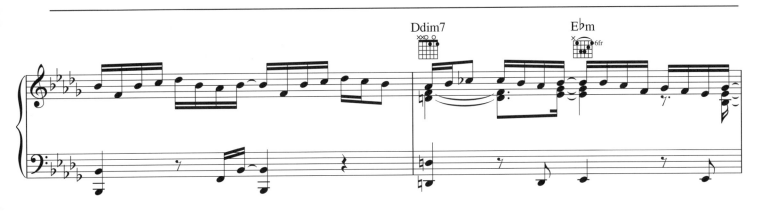

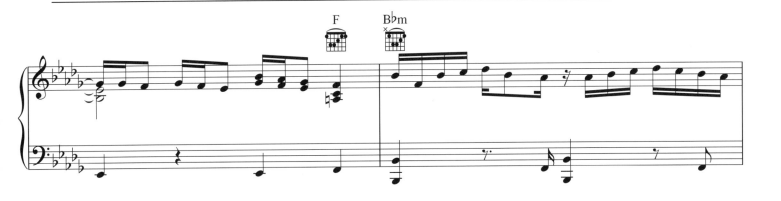

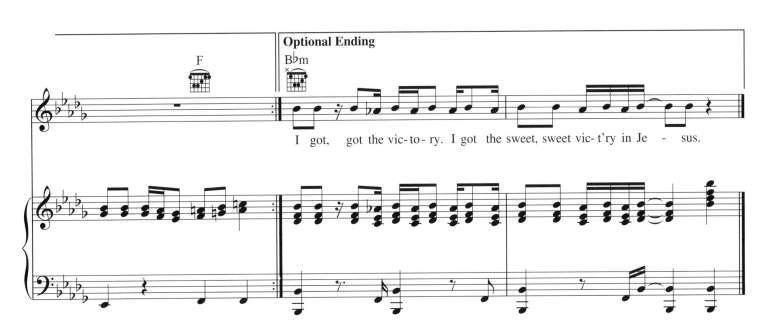

I got, got the vic-to-ry. I got the sweet, sweet vic-t'ry in Je - sus.

GLORIOUS

Words and Music by ISRAEL HOUGHTON
and MARTHA MUNIZZI

YOU ARE GOOD

Words and Music by
ISRAEL HOUGHTON

So good, so good. Yes, You are. Yes, You are. Yes, You are.

You are __ good __ all the time. __

__ All the time, __ You are __ good. __ You are __ good __

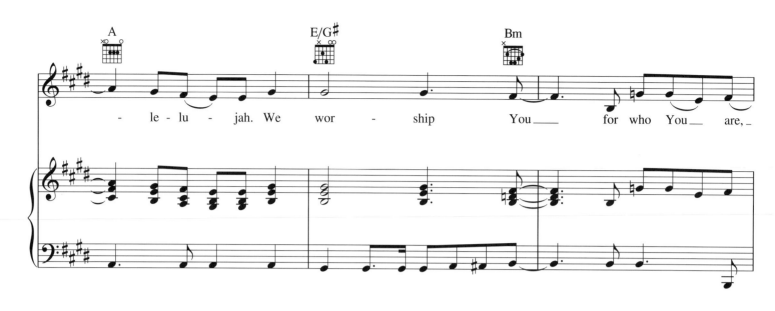

STILL ALIVE

Words and Music by
KIRK FRANKLIN

God is a good God and His love en - dur - eth. Be -

A CHANGE IS GONNA COME

Words and Music by
SAM COOKE

I was born by the riv - er
It's been too hard for liv - ing,
Then I go to the mov - ie,

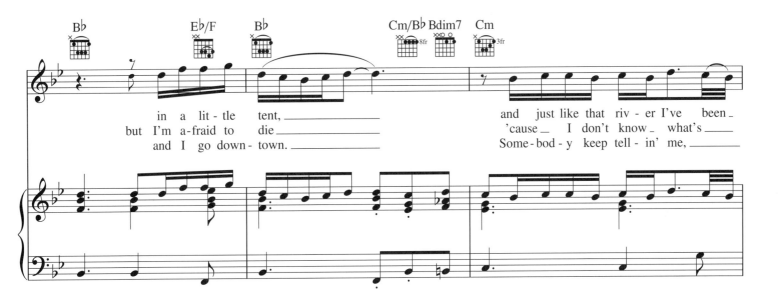

in a lit - tle tent, _____ and just like that riv - er I've been _____
but I'm a - fraid to die _____ 'cause _____ I don't know _____ what's _____
and I go down - town. _____ Some - bod - y keep tell - in' me, _____

run - ning _____ ev - er, _____ ev - er since.
up there _____ be - yond _____ the sky. It's been a
_____ "don't ya, _____ don't ya hang a - round."

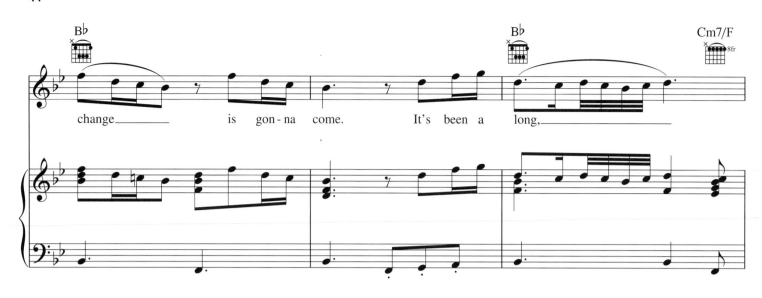

change_____ is gon-na come. It's been a long,_____

a long____ time____ com - ing,____ but I know_____ a

Freely

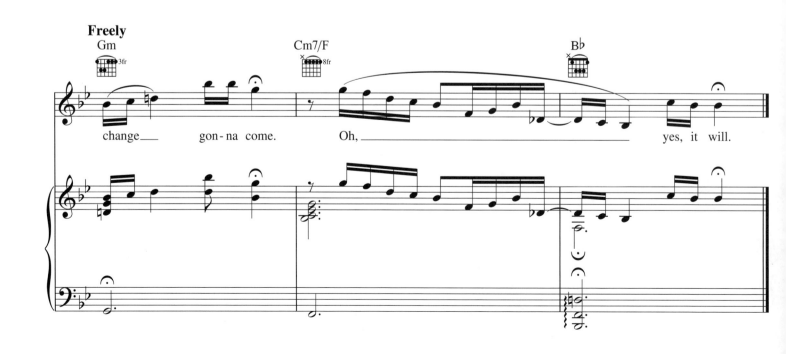

change____ gon-na come. Oh,_____ yes, it will.

OOH CHILD

Words and Music by
STAN VINCENT

<tt>50</tt>

Rap Lyrics

If you're tired of the crying, come on.
If you're tired of people dying, come on.
If you're tired of the fighting, come on.
No more wars, no more lying, come on.

All my people in the world, come on.
Every boy, every girl, come on.
If you know it ain't over 'til God says that it's over,
Come on, well, come on, let's go!

THE CLOSER I GET TO YOU

Words and Music by JAMES MTUME
and REGGIE LUCAS

Slowly

mp

Dmaj9   C#m7 F#m7 Amaj7

Dmaj9   C#m7 F#m7 Amaj7

Dmaj9   C#m7 F#m7

Girls: The clos-er I get to you,

Amaj7   Dmaj9   C#m7   F#m7

the more you make me ___ see. ___

Amaj7   Dmaj9   C#m7   F#m7

By giv-ing me all you've got, ___

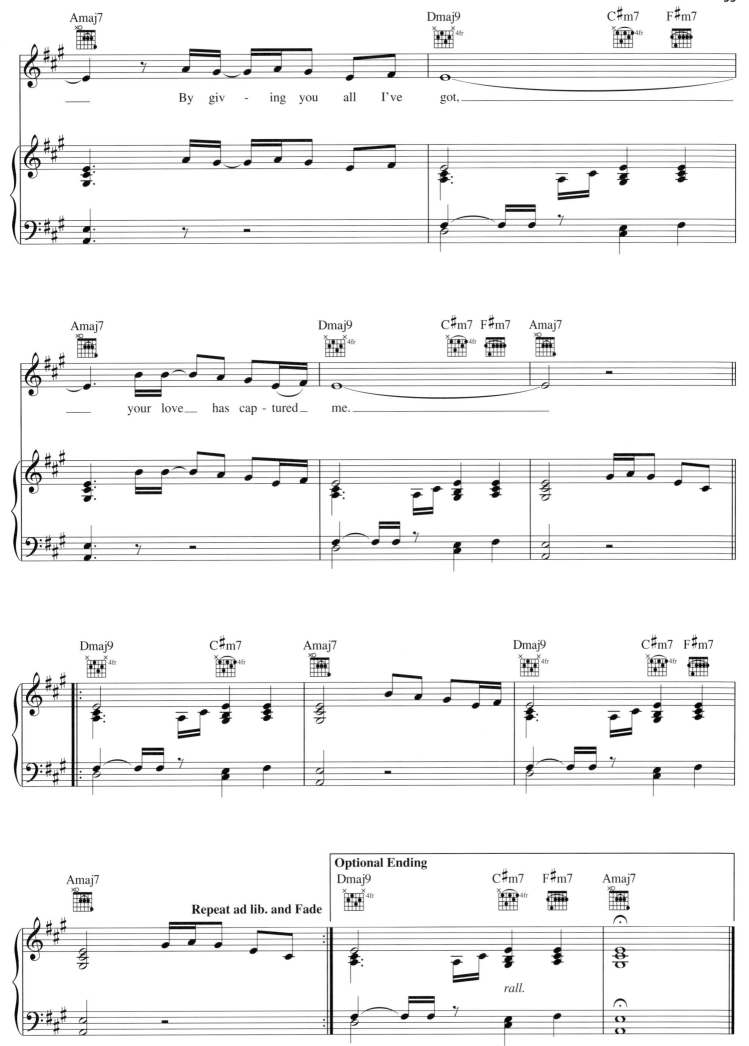

WHEN I PRAY (INTERLUDE)

Words and Music by JOANN ROSARIO
and ZABDIEL BELLO GONZALEZ

Yes, I know that You can hear me. And I feel You

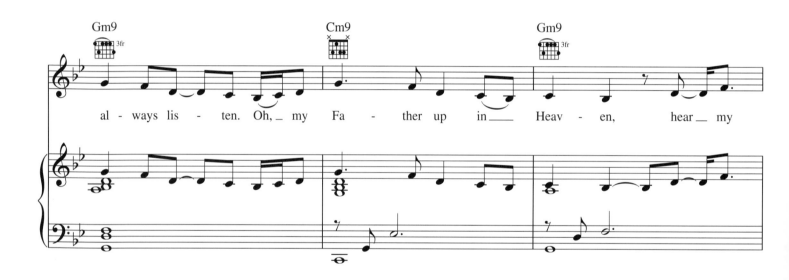

al - ways lis - ten. Oh, my Fa - ther up in Heav - en, hear my

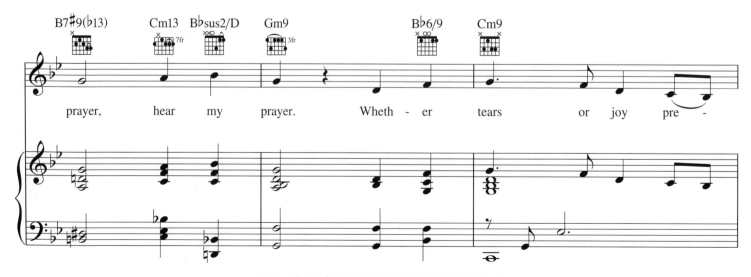

prayer, hear my prayer. Wheth - er tears or joy pre -

ALL THINGS ARE WORKING

Words and Music by FRED HAMMOND,
TOMMIE WALKER and KIM RUTHERFORD

I NEED YOU TO SURVIVE

Words and Music by
DAVID FRAZIER

NOW BEHOLD THE LAMB

Words and Music by
KIRK FRANKLIN

PUT YOUR HANDS TOGETHER

Words and Music by KENNETH GAMBLE
and LEON HUFF